Studies and Melodious Etudes for Alto Saxophone

LEVEL THREE
(ADVANCED INTERMEDIATE)

by
Willis Coggins
in collaboration with
James Ployhar

To the Teacher

"Studies And Melodious Etudes", Level III, is a supplementary technic book of the Belwin "STUDENT INSTRUMENTAL COURSE". Although planned as a companion and correlating book of the method, "The Alto Saxophone Student", it can also be used effectively with most intermediate or advanced alto saxophone instruction books. It provides for extended and additional treatment in technical areas, which are limited in the basic method because of lack of space. Emphasis is on developing musicianship through scales, warm-ups and technical drills, musicianship studies and interesting melody-like etudes.

The Belwin "STUDENT INSTRUMENTAL COURSE" - A course for individual and class instruction of LIKE instruments, at three levels, for all band instruments.

EACH BOOK IS COMPLETE IN ITSELF BUT ALL BOOKS ARE CORRELATED WITH EACH OTHER

METHOD
"The Alto Saxophone Student"
For Individual
or E♭ Saxophone Class Instruction.

ALTHOUGH EACH BOOK CAN BE USED SEPARATELY, IDEALLY, ALL SUPPLEMENTARY BOOKS SHOULD BE USED AS COMPANION BOOKS WITH THE METHOD

STUDIES & MELODIOUS ETUDES

Supplementary scales, warm-up and technical drills, musicianship studies and melody-like etudes, all carefully correlated with the method.

TUNES FOR TECHNIC

Technical type melodies, variations, and "famous passages" from musical literature for the development of technical dexterity.

ALTO SAXOPHONE SOLOS

Four separate correlated Solos, with piano accompaniment, selected, written or arranged by Willis Coggins:

Matador . . . . *Girlamo*
Gigue . . . . *Corelli*
Cantilena . . . . . . *Fredrickson*
Romance No. I . . . . *Schumann*

CORRELATED SAXOPHONE SOLOS

Four separate solos, with piano accompaniment, were selected and arranged specifically for this course. We strongly encourage the use of these solos as supplementary lesson material.

MATADOR .... Robert Girlamo
       ed. by Willis Coggins
GIGUE........................ Arcangelo Corelli
       arr. by Willis Coggins

CANTILENA .... Thomas Fredrickson
       ed. by Willis Coggins
ROMANCE NO. I .... Robert Schumann
       arr. by Willis Coggins

SAXOPHONE FINGERING CHART

When a number is given, refer to the picture of the Saxophone for additional keys to be pressed. When two notes are given together (F♯ and G♭) they are the same tone and, of course, played the same way.

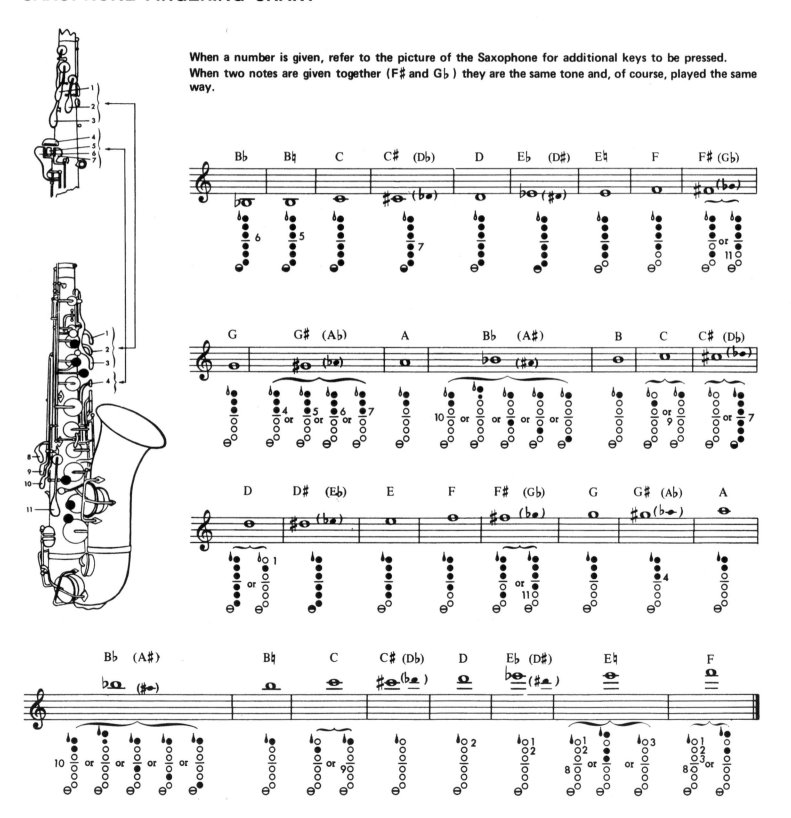

Vibrato

Vibrato is a pulsation of the tone which is accompanied by a slight change of pitch. It is produced on the saxophone by a small, up-and down, chewing motion of the jaw.

First say to-wo-wo-wo without the mouthpiece, and notice the amount of jaw movement. Then, make the same movement while playing a long tone on the instrument. Next, move the jaw rhythmically at a rate of four pulsations per beat. Also, see page 3 of The Alto Saxophone Student, Level three.

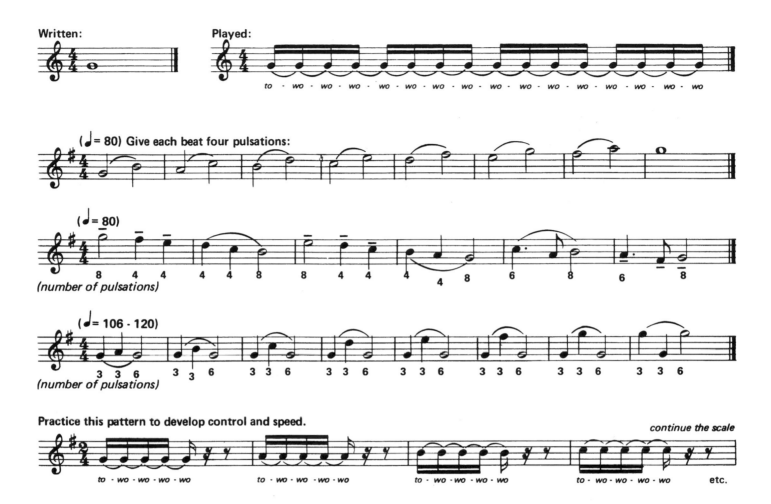

Practice this pattern to develop control and speed.

DAILY WARM-UP STUDIES

Practice with and without vibrato.

4

C Major scale in thirds

ABBREVIATION STUDIES

Written: *Sempre staccato*

Played:

Written: *Sempre staccato*

Played:

Etude No. 1

Polonaise

KLOSÉ

Allegretto

a tempo

poco rit.

C Major Arpeggio

A Minor Arpeggio

A Minor Scale (in thirds)

Compare these two lines:

Play the different rhythms accurately.

Etude No. 2

Moderato

mf

B.I.C.332

Tenuto and Slurred Tenuto: Lightly tongue each note and play full value. Play slurred tenuto notes more connected than tenuto notes.

Semi- Staccato (Half-Staccato): Tongue each note and shorten slightly with the breath.

RHYTHM STUDY - Sharp Staccato (▾ ▾ ▾ ▾)

Compare the rhythms in measures 1 & 2.

Etude No. 3

Tango

E Minor

Accent Marks

When written: >>>>, emphasize each note, decrease its loudness, and shorten it slightly.   When written: ∧∧∧∧, emphasize each note, but keep the loudness for the duration of the note.

Slurred Accents (>>>>)

Emphasize each note, decrease its loudness, but do not separate.

Andante

RHYTHM STUDY   Same:

1   2 3   1   23

Etude No. 4

BROD

Andante sostenuto (♪= 104)

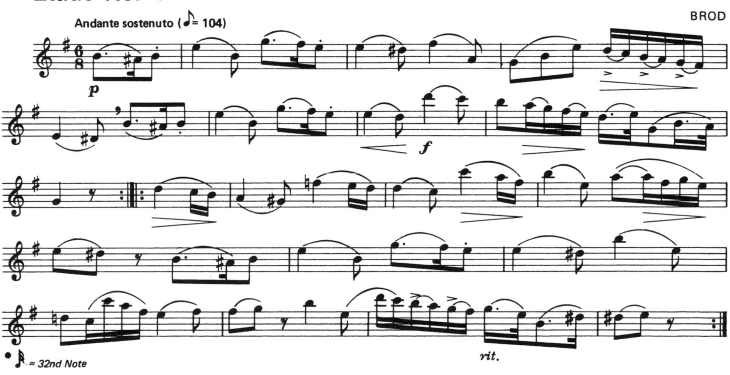

*♪ = 32nd Note   rit.

F Major Studies

BROD

Prelude

CAVALLINI

ABBREVIATIONS

[∕.] — means: Repeat the preceeding measure.　　[∕.] — means: Repeat the 2 preceeding measures.

(Play ∧ short and accented)

Etude No. 5

BARRET

D Minor Studies

(Thirds)

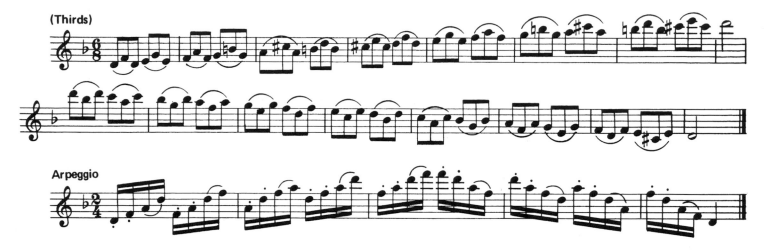

Arpeggio

THE DOUBLE-DOTTED QUARTER NOTE

ABBREVIATIONS

Etude No. 6

D Major Arpeggio Study

TIME AND 6/4 TIME

Count: 1 2 3 4 5 6
1   2

THE GRACE NOTE (♪)

Play before the beat, just ahead of the principal note (accented note). It may appear as single, double, triple, or quadruple notation.

Written:

Played:

Etude No. 7

Tempo di Valz

BROD

Fine

D. S. al Fine

Keeping one or more right hand fingers down often facilitates changing registers:

TONGUING STUDY

MAZAS

DOUBLE - DOTTED HALF NOTES:

Etude No. 8

BERR

B Minor Arpeggio Study

THE APPOGGIATURA

The appoggiatura is a melodic ornament which borrows from the principal note the time necessary for its performance: half value, or in the case of a dotted note, two-thirds of its value.   (Also see page 15 of The Alto Saxophone Student)

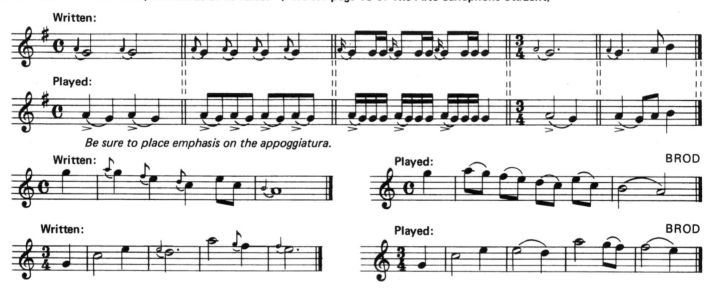

Be sure to place emphasis on the appoggiatura.

Etude No. 9

TRILL STUDIES

Etude No. 10

B♭ Major

(In thirds)

Arpeggio Study

Etude No. 11

SYNCOPATION STUDIES

G Minor Arpeggio Study

(In thirds)

THE TURN (GRUPETTO)

Written: Also Written: Played:

Etude No. 12

KLOSÉ

Allegretto

mp

mf

a tempo

rit.

ALTERNATE FINGERINGS

High F

High E (no. 2)

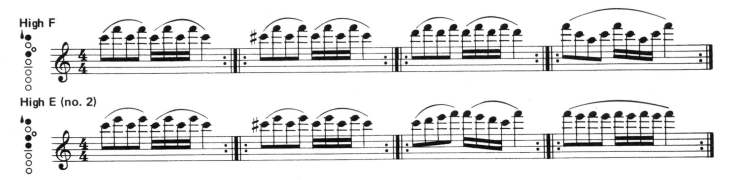

TURN SIGN DIRECTLY OVER A NOTE

Written:　　　　　　　　Played:

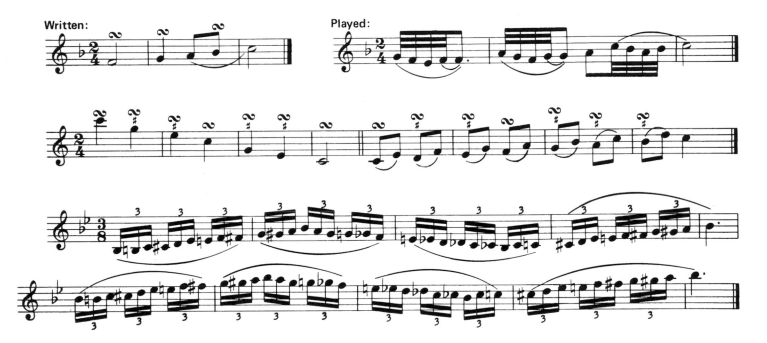

Etude No. 13

Moderato

ALTERNATE FINGERING

High E (no. 3)

When a turn sign is placed after a dotted note:

Played:

Moderato

KLOSÉ

Fine

D. C. al Fine

Etude No. 14

Moderato

*Use alternate high F fingering.
(2) & (3) — Alternate high E fingerings. (See fingering chart.)

Eb Major (in thirds)

Arpeggios

THE INVERTED TURN (∽)

(When written after the note) Play: (When written over the note) Play

Etude No. 15

SPOHR

Allegretto

C Minor Arpeggio Study

TRIPLET STUDIES

(Thirds)

TRIPLETS IN ¢ TIME

Etude No. 16

BARRET

A Major
(Thirds)

Arpeggio

REVIEW OF EMBELLISHMENTS

Etude No. 17

Allegro

H. BROD

F# Minor

SIXTEENTH REST STUDY

Keep key 7 open   Keep key 5   Keep key 6   Keep key 7

Keep key 7 . . . .   (Do not keep key 7 open) . . . .

Etude No. 18

Waltz tempo

f

SIXTEENTH REST STUDY

Ab Major

COMPOUND TIME STUDY

THE MORDENT ( ).   Rapidly alternate between the principal note and the tone below.

Written: Played:

THE INVERTED MORDENT.   Short trill. ( ).   Rapidly alternate between the principal note and the tone above

Written: Played:

ARBAN

Etude No. 19

Allegro moderato

BLATT

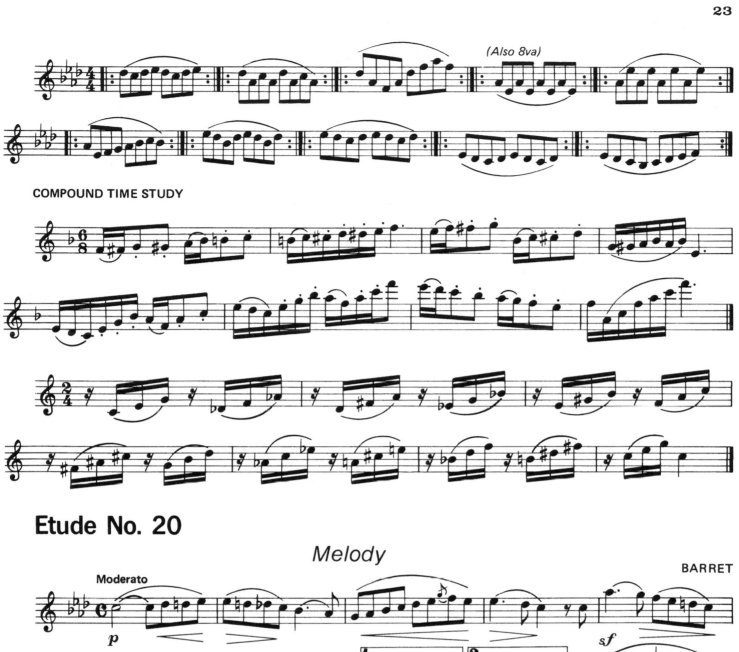

COMPOUND TIME STUDY

Etude No. 20

Melody

BARRET

F Minor (in thirds)

COMPOUND TIME STUDIES

Etude No. 21

Siciliano

KLOSÉ

SELLNER

16TH REST STUDY

SYNCOPATION STUDY

Etude No. 22

Allegretto

E Major
Arpeggios

(Thirds)

TIME SIGNATURE STUDY

Etude No. 23

Moderato

mf

KLOSÉ

FINGERING STUDIES

Keep F♯/G♭ plate closed

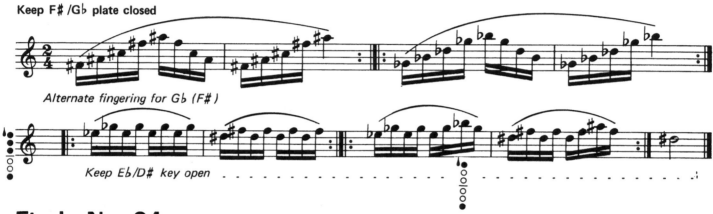

Alternate fingering for G♭ (F♯)

Keep E♭/D♯ key open ‑

Etude No. 24

BLATT

Allegro con brio

Like G♮

C# MINOR

(Arpeggios)

(Thirds)

SYNCOPATION IN ₵

RHYTHM STUDY

Etude No. 25

SPOHR

Etude No. 26

Syncopation Etude

Etude No. 27

Petite Etude

BARRET

Db MAJOR

(Arpeggio)

(Thirds)

Keep key 7 open *Key F# plate closed* *Keep key 4 open* *Keep key 4 open* *Keep R.H. Fingers*

COMPOUND TIME STUDY

Etude No. 28

Moderato

KLOSÉ

Fine

D. C. al Fine

CHROMATIC ARPEGGIO STUDY

COMPOUND TIME

Etude No. 29

Moderato

KLOSÉ

Etude No. 30

Scherzo

Allegro

FERLING